Contents

A Note From the Executive Director

100 years in the hospitality industry is a long time. Considering that most restaurants fail in their first three years of operation, a Centennial is truly a time for celebration. I cannot think of a better way to mark the Campus Club's 100th anniversary than with a cookbook, acknowledging that the Club brings together members of the University community around good food and drink.

The food prepared at the Campus Club is fresh and healthful. Our bread is baked daily with local, organic flour. The dressings, sauces, jams, and chutneys that accompany and flavor our entrées and salads are made in the Club kitchen from scratch. Many of the ingredients are local, for freshness and quality, but also to highlight Minnesota-developed varieties of fruits and vegetables; cheeses made by the students at the University Dairy Lab, and produce grown especially for the Campus Club by the students at Cornercopia, the student organic farm. I like to think of the Campus Club as a place to showcase the best regional flavors applied to world cuisine.

There is a lot of variety in this cookbook. The recipes presented here are a small selection of the many original dishes that Chef Beth Jones has come up with during her time as Executive Chef, but they are a good representation of what is served daily at the Campus Club. They are adapted for home use. Enjoy them!

Ann Holt
Executive Director

Acknowledgements

This is the first cookbook put together by the Campus Club in its 100 year history. It has been an exciting project, and would not have come together without the help of some key individuals who were willing to put in much time and effort to make it happen. Our thanks to:

Beth Jones, Campus Club Executive Chef, for compiling, writing and testing the recipes, organizing and supervising the photography. Beth is a rare individual who has many talents, and the Campus Club truly benefits from her love of cooking and teaching, her tenacity, and willingness to take on new projects.

Jorge Ortega, Campus Club Sous Chef, for assisting Beth in writing, testing, and contributing his own recipes. Thanks also to Jorge for keeping the kitchen running smoothly while Beth took time away to plan the cookbook.

Joe Burgmeier, Photographer, for taking all the beautiful photographs in this book. While employed at the Campus Club as a server, bartender, graphics guy, and photographer, Joe was also a full time student at Art Institutes International, Minnesota.

Mark Hoey, Project Supervisor, for all his work pulling the various pieces together, designing the layout, and organizing the copy. Mark gave our ideas and intentions for the book balance, beauty and a coherence we had not imagined. Mark is an architect by training, and we feel so lucky he was able to take on this project.

The Campus Club Board of Directors, for trusting us to pursue this project in spite of the fact that we had no budget and no experience in publishing.

The members of the Campus Club, who insist upon healthful, flavorful and interesting cuisine, and who ask again and again for recipes.

Sincerely,

Ann Holt
Executive Director

Phil Platt
Marketing and Membership Director

A Note From the Executive Chef

It's hard to explain the way we cook at the Campus Club. Most restaurants start with a set menu, order the ingredients, and follow a recipe for preparing a dish. Same dish, no matter what, every time you order it. But here at the Club, we look at what local farmers are offering every week, order what's seasonal, affordable, interesting, or simply what we happen to be craving that day, and make it up as we go along. That makes writing recipes extremely difficult. What I've assembled in this book are the basic guidelines for making many of the favorite dishes we serve at the Club. When you're cooking from this book, take the recipes as suggestions, not as law. Go to the Church Street Farmer's Market, the local co-ops, or look in your CSA box, and throw in what's good, fresh, and local and adapt these recipes to the seasons. Your food will taste better, and you'll have more fun cooking it. We certainly do!

Beth Jones
Executive Chef

When using these recipes:
- *large dice = 1" square*
- *medium dice = 1/2" square*
- *small dice = 1/4" square*

Board of Directors Message

"'Eating together,' as Dr. Johnson would say, 'promotes good will, sir; commensality is benevolent.'" The remark is a journalist's apt invention. What Samuel Johnson did say he said in his famous Dictionary (1755), giving the hard word commensality a crisp definition: "Fellowship of table; the custom of eating together." Other dictionaries kept this latent word on call for more than a century, until it was finally adopted and put to use by jurists and anthropologists. Mensa was the Latin word for table; and those who shared a table were understood to establish a community that was more than a matter of meat and drink.

It was to make such community for the University of Minnesota that the founders of the Campus Club gathered round its tables a century ago. The same goal still engages the board of directors, who meet over lunch each month to plan the future of the Club into its second century.

Commensality presupposes good food. Quite a few fine meals have been had at the Campus Club over the past century, and the pages that follow recall or renew some of them. Do try these recipes at home; commensality begins at home. The Campus Club is a home for all members and friends of the University. Welcome to the table.

Board of Directors, The Campus Club

John Finnegan, *President*
Lincoln Kallsen, *Vice-President*

Suzanne Bardouche, *Secretary*
Mike Rollefson, *Treasurer*

John Adams	Kate Maple	Karen Zentner Bacig
S. Massoud Amin	Ann S. Masten	Ex Officio
Gary B. Cohen	Meredith McQuaid	Kim Munholland
Michael Hancher	Abel Ponce de Leon	Ann Holt
Robert J. Jones	Henning Schroeder	Ann Hill Duin

Local Vendors

1) **Callister Farm,** *West Concord, MN*
   Free range chicken and eggs
   Available at the St. Paul Farmer's Market, and local Co-ops
   www.callisterfarm.com

2) **Classic Provisions,** *Plymouth, MN*
   Locally sourced cheeses, meats, and gourmet products
   763-544-2025
   www.classicprovisions.com

3) **Coastal Seafoods,** *Minneapolis, MN*
   Sustainably sourced fish, seafood, and meats
   612-724-7425
   www.coastalseafoods.com

4) **Co-op Partners,** *St Paul, MN*
   Local and organic produce, grains, and flour
   Products available at local Co-ops
   www.cooppartners.coop

5) **Cornercopia,** *St. Paul, MN*
   Fruits, vegetables, and herbs
   Available at the Church Street Farmer's Market
   http://sof.cfans.umn.edu/

6) **Ferndale Market**, *Cannon Falls, MN*
   Free-range, naturally processed turkey
   Available at Ferndale Market, and Seward Co-op
   www.ferndalemarketonline.com

7) **Hidden Stream Farm,** *Elgin, MN*
   Fruits, vegetables, pork, chicken, and eggs
   Available at local Co-ops
   507-876-2304
   www.hiddenstreamfarm.com

8) Hill and Vale Farm, *Wykoff, MN*
Grass-fed lamb and beef
Available at Seward Co-op
www.localharvest.org/hill-and-vale-farms-M3390

9) Hope Creamery, *Hope, MN*
Cream, butter, milk, and eggs
Available at local Co-ops

10) Riverbend Farm, *Delano, MN*
Vegetables and herbs
Available for CSA shares and at local Co-ops
www.rbfcsa.com

11) Star Prairie Trout Farm, *Star Prairie, WI*
Fresh and smoked trout, available at Coastal Seafoods stores and the Mill City Farmers Market
www.starprairietrout.com

12) Tim Fischer, *Waseca, MN*
Hormone-free pork
Available at Local D'Lish
www.fischerfamilyfarmspork.com

13) Local D'Lish, *Minneapolis, MN*
Local meats, cheeses, produce, and breads
612-886-3047
www.localdlish.com

14) Seward Coop, *Minneapolis, MN*
Locally sourced meats, fish, and produce
612-338-2465
www.seward.coop

15) Southeast MN Food Network, *Elgin, MN*
Produce, meat, poultry, and honey
Available at local Co-ops
www.southeastmnfood.com

16) Stonebridge Beef, *Long Prairie, MN*
Grass-fed beef
Available direct from the farm
320-594-0031

17) Thousand Hills Cattle Company, *Cannon Falls, MN*
Grass-fed, Midwestern beef
Available at local Co-ops and Ferndale Market
www.thousandhillscattleco.com

18) U of M Dairy Plant, *St. Paul, MN*
University-made cheeses, meats, and ice cream
http://fscn.cfans.umn.edu/researchandservices/dairysalesroom/

19) U of M Arboretum, *Chaska, MN*
University of Minnesota developed apples
952-443-1400
www.arboretum.umn.edu

20) Whole Farm Coop, *Long Prairie, MN*
Local grains, produce, and honey
Products available online
320-732-3023
www.wholefarmcoop.com

University of Minnesota Products

Cornercopia Student Organic Farm
St. Paul Campus
http://sof.cfans.umn.edu/

As a chef, I feel extremely blessed to have Cornercopia, and in particular, it's coordinator, Courtney Tchida, available to me as a source for amazing, organically grown food, and information about it. Cornercopia is a student driven and run, certified organic farm on the St. Paul Campus, that grows over 100 varieties of fruits and vegetables. Their goal is to give students the opportunity to learn first-hand what it takes to plan, grow, and market food. I first met Courtney Tchida in the winter of 2008, when she and several of her students approached us about buying produce. I came to that meeting with a huge wish list of things for them to grow, and over the next three years they have delivered a greater variety of amazing fruits and vegetables than I could have ever imagined. In addition to great food, Cornercopia has provided me with a greater appreciation for the work and dedication it takes to coax a seed into a gorgeous organic tomato. Courtney and I have worked together on a number of projects including the, "Locavore 101," classes we teach at the Campus Club. Our partnership with Cornercopia has been one of the most enjoyable parts of my job as Executive Chef. Courtney is responsible for training a new generation of organic farmers that are changing the food culture in our community, and having the opportunity to support her efforts makes my job even more rewarding.

University Dairy Plant
St. Paul Campus
http://fscn.cfans.umn.edu/research-andservices/dairysalesroom/

The Campus Club has been buying fabulous cheeses from the University Dairy Plant since long before I became chef. Over the course of a year we go through hundreds of pounds of the University's cheddar, pepper jack, gouda, and especially the amazing Minnesota Blue, which we use to make the Campus Club Blue Cheese Dressing. In the summer of 2009, while I was 6 months pregnant, Ann Holt, Sous Chef Jorge Ortega, and I took a day-long class at the plant on cheese-making, taught by Ray Miller, Jodi Nelson, and Tonya Schoenfuss. We spent the day hand pulling fresh mozzarella, making herbed feta, and watching a hot-tub sized vat of milk being made into huge blocks of cheddar cheese. At the end of the day I was absolutely exhausted, but I came away with a new appreciation for the amount of time and effort it takes to make a huge amount of milk into a small amount of cheese. No crumb gets wasted in our kitchen! The University's cheeses are featured on our cheese platters for catered events and are used in many other dishes we make at the Club. The Dairy Store sells items that are produced in the Dairy Plant by students, faculty and staff. The products are made during classes and research projects, or are produced during breaks as a way to fund research and maintenance of the facility. The Dairy Food Products Salesroom is open to the public on Wednesdays from 3-5 p.m. It is located in Room 166 Andrew Boss Lab of Meat Science (ABLMS), 1354 Eckles Avenue, St. Paul Campus. In addition to cheeses, the store offers a variety of meats and ice cream. Get there early if you want their cheese curds!

Minnesota Landscape Arboretum
3675 Arboretum Drive
Chaska MN 55318
http://www.arboretum.umn.edu/

Our partnership with the Arboretum has several different components. In the fall they sell us apples which we use in our kitchen and sell directly to our members. They have participated in our Oktoberfest events, organizing apple tastings and allowing our guests to sample many different varieties, new releases, and old favorites. We also take our turn in the Arboretum's beautiful venue during the annual Toast and Taste in the gardens, a showcase event for Twin Cities restaurants that use local foods. In 2009 and 2010 our front of the house manager, Katherine Zimmerman, who is a trained pastry chef, participated in the Arboretum's Land of Gingerbread exhibit in the Oswald Visitor Center, with two amazing gingerbread villages.

The Lounge Corridor, suitable for receptions, is adjacent to the Terrace and overlooks the Mall.

Appetizers

U of M Blue Cheese Stuffed Dates

This may be the easiest recipe in this book, and yet the flavors are so amazing that your guests will think you slaved over this! You can buy the blue cheese on the St. Paul campus on Wednesdays in the Dairy Store. Dairy Food Products Salesroom is open to the public on Wednesdays from 3-5 p.m. It is located in Room 166 Andrew Boss Lab of Meat Science (ABLMS), 1354 Eckles Avenue, St. Paul Campus

24 whole dates
6 ounces Minnesota Blue Cheese

Makes 24

Preheat oven to 375. Using a paring knife, make a small slit across the length of each date. Remove the pits, and stuff each with a piece of the cheese. Place the dates on a baking sheet, and bake for 5 minutes.

Serve immediately.

Beet-Dyed Deviled Eggs

I first invented these eggs in the Spring of 2010 to serve at the reception for the School of Public Health's film festival, featuring the movie, "Food Fight." I was honored to be included in the panel discussion following the movie, but my favorite part of the evening may have been people's reactions to these eggs! One excited little girl even asked me if they were candy!

2 large beets, peeled and diced small
6 cups water
1 Tablespoon white vinegar

1 dozen hard boiled eggs
2 teaspoons grainy mustard
2 Tablespoons mayonnaise
2 teaspoons chives, minced
A dash of Tabasco
Salt and pepper to taste
1 cup assorted micro-greens

Makes 24

Boil the beets in the water for 15 minutes, or until tender. Remove the beets from the liquid and save for another use. Cool the liquid and add the vinegar.

Cut the eggs in half lengthwise and remove the yolks. Soak the egg whites in the beet liquid for 1-3 hours, depending on how deeply you want the whites to be dyed.

Mix the yolks with the mustard, mayo, Tabasco, salt and pepper. Remove the egg whites from the beet liquid and blot dry with a paper towel. Spoon the yolk mixture back into the egg whites, and garnish each with a generous sprig of micro-greens.

Patacones with Shrimp

We first served these fried plantains at the Ecuadorian Buffet that the Club held in 2008. Sous Chef Jorge Ortega designed the menu and included these as an appetizer, and they have since become one of our best-sellers both in the bar, and on our catering menu.

Makes 24

Mayo
1 cup mayonnaise
Juice and zest from 1 lemon
1 teaspoon sriracha, or other hot sauce

Plantains
4 green plantains
1 quart vegetable oil
Salt and pepper to taste

Shrimp
24 large shrimp, peeled and deveined
1 ½ teaspoons sriracha, or other hot sauce
1 Tablespoon canola oil
¼ cup chopped cilantro
2 avocadoes, sliced

Mix the mayonnaise, lemon juice, and hot sauce and set aside.

Preheat the oven to 150. Peel the plantains, and cut into 1- inch rounds. Heat the oil in a large heavy pot, to 325. Fry the plantains in batches until golden, about 3-5 minutes per batch. Remove the plantains and set on a paper towel. Allow to cool slightly. Using the bottom of a heavy drinking glass, flatten each plantain to about 1/8 inch thickness. Check the oil temperature, and refry the plantains for another 3-5 minutes, or until golden brown. Allow to drain on new paper towels, and sprinkle lightly with salt and pepper. Hold the plantains in the oven until ready to serve.

Toss the shrimp with the oil and hot sauce, and sprinkle lightly with salt and pepper. Grill the shrimp for 1-2 minutes per side. Top each plantain with a bit of the mayo, and one shrimp. Sprinkle with cilantro and serve with sliced avocado.

Tomato Basil Bruschetta

This recipe is best saved for August and September when there is an abundance of local tomatoes to be had. Have fun and use a big mix of varieties, shapes and colors. In 2010 Cornercopia planted 28 different types of tomatoes. My favorite are the tiny little currant tomatoes, which pack a load of sugar and flavor into a tiny, beautiful little package. Look for them each year at the Church Street Farmer's Market.

2 cups mixed variety tomatoes, small dice, or cut in half if small

1 Tablespoon red onion, minced

1 small clove garlic, minced

2 Tablespoons basil, chiffonade

1 Tablespoon capers

5 pitted kalamata olives, chopped

3 Tablespoons good quality olive oil

Pinch of salt, and freshly ground black pepper

4 ounces goat cheese (I prefer Donnay Chevre, from Kimball, MN)

1 baguette, sliced into ½ inch rounds

Olive oil for brushing

¼ cup grated parmesan

Makes about 25 bruschettas

Mix the first 8 ingredients together in a medium bowl, and allow to sit for one hour.

Preheat the broiler. Arrange the baguette slices on a cookie sheet and brush with olive oil. Toast the bread under the broiler for 30 seconds, or until brown. The bread could also be grilled if desired.

Spread each toast with goat cheese, and top with the tomato mixture. Sprinkle with the parmesan and serve immediately.

Note: To chiffonade basil, or other herbs, lay whole leaves on top of each other and roll lengthwise into a cigarette shape. Using a sharp chef's knife, cut thin strips across the rolled leaves. Toss the strips to separate, and add to your dish.

Hummus

1- 24 ounce can chickpeas, liquid reserved

2 cloves garlic

Juice and zest from 1 lemon

½ cup olive oil

Salt and pepper to taste

Makes about 2 cups

Purée the chickpeas, garlic, lemon zest and juice in the bowl of a food processor. With the motor running, drizzle in the olive oil. Add enough of the reserved liquid to reach desired consistency.

Season to taste with salt and pepper, and serve with fresh veggies and flatbread for dipping.

Seafood Empanadas

Makes 20, 4-inch empanadas

Shrimp and Crab Filling

1-10 ounce can backfin crabmeat

6 ounces cream cheese

1 jalepeño, grilled and seeded, small dice

1 cup mini salad shrimp

Gently mix the crabmeat with the cream cheese and jalepeño. The shrimp will be added later.

Chimichurri Sauce

1 bunch cilantro with stems, roughly chopped

1 bunch parsley with stems, roughly chopped

1 large clove garlic

1 teaspoon Tabasco

½ cup olive oil

2 Tablespoons water

Salt and pepper to taste

For the chimichurri sauce, blend all ingredients in the bowl of a food processor until smooth.

Empanada Dough

2 ½ cups flour

1 stick butter (cold), cut into small pieces

1 teaspoon sugar

1 teaspoon salt

1 egg

½ cup ice water

6 cups canola oil for frying

For the dough, mix the dry ingredients in a food processor. Add the butter and pulse to form a coarse meal. Add the egg, and pulse. With the motor running, drizzle in the water and process just until the dough holds together. Form the dough into a flat round, wrap with plastic, and chill for one hour.

When the dough is chilled, flour a flat surface and roll out into a thin sheet. Using a 4-inch round cutter, cut out 20 rounds. Any leftover dough can be re-rolled for more empanadas.

. . . continued on page 30

. . . continued from page 29

Fill each empanada with 2 table-spoons of the crab filling and 2 or 3 shrimp. Fold the empanadas in half, brush the edge with water and seal with the tines of a fork. If you are preparing the empanadas ahead of time, they may be frozen on a sheet tray at this point, and fried later.

If preparing immediately, heat 6 cups of oil to 325 in a heavy, deep pot. Fry the empanadas in batch-es for 3-5 minutes until golden brown. Drain on a paper towel and serve with the chimichurri sauce.

The Dale Shephard Room is perfect for private dinners, meetings, and intimate functions.

Dressings and Salads

U of M Blue Cheese Dressing

1 cup buttermilk

1 cup sour cream

1 Tablespoon fresh lemon juice

1 ½ teaspoons champagne vinegar

½ pound crumbled Minnesota blue cheese

Salt and pepper to taste

Makes 2 ½ cups

Whisk together all the ingredients except the blue cheese. Crumble the cheese into small chunks and stir into the dressing. Season to taste with salt and pepper.

Italian Vinaigrette

1 teaspoon whole fennel seed
1 small clove garlic, minced
¼ cup red wine vinegar
3 Tablespoons water
1 Tablespoon Dijon mustard
½ teaspoon dried oregano
½ teaspoon dried basil
¾ cup olive oil

Makes about 2 cups

In a small sauté pan, over medium heat, toast the fennel seeds until fragrant. Grind the fennel in a spice grinder. In the bowl of a blender or food processor combine the garlic, vinegar, water, mustard, and spices. Slowly drizzle the olive oil into the mixture. Season to taste with salt and pepper.

Campus Club Thousand Island Dressing

1 cup mayonnaise
½ cup buttermilk
⅓ cup ketchup
⅓ cup finely diced pickled beets
1 teaspoon lemon zest
1 Tablespoon fresh lemon juice
¼ teaspoon paprika
½ teaspoon Tabasco sauce
Salt and pepper to taste

Makes 2 ½ cups

Whisk together all ingredients and refrigerate one hour before using.

Honey Thyme Vinaigrette

1 Tablespoon honey

1 Tablespoon plus 1 teaspoon fresh thyme leaves, minced

2 Tablespoons cider vinegar

2 Tablespoons apple cider

1 Tablespoon grainy mustard

¼ cup olive oil

½ cup canola oil

Pinch of salt and freshly ground black pepper

Makes about 1½ cups

In a small bowl, whisk together the honey, thyme, vinegar, cider, and mustard. Slowly drizzle in the two oils. Thin the dressing with a few drops of water if necessary, and season to taste with salt and freshly ground black pepper.

Balsamic Vermont Cranberry Bean Salad

For the Vinaigrette
3 Tablespoons balsamic vinegar
1 Tablespoon Dijon mustard
2 cloves garlic minced
½ cup extra virgin olive oil

For the Salad
3 cups Vermont Cranberry beans, cooked
¼ cup minced red onion
½ cup sundried tomatoes, julienne
½ cup fresh basil, chiffonade
Salt and pepper to taste

Serves 4

In a small bowl, mix the vinegar, mustard, and garlic. Slowly drizzle in the olive oil, whisking to emulsify.

In a medium bowl, mix the beans, onion, sundried tomatoes, and vinaigrette. Let the salad marinate for at least an hour, but preferably overnight. Add the basil just before serving and season to taste with salt and freshly ground black pepper.

Greg's Swedish Brown Beans with Dill

I first made this salad for an Arboretum event featuring Michael Pollan, author of, "The Omnivore's Dilemma." I was a bit nervous about how much local food I'd be able to find in early April, but there was plenty available, including beautiful dried Swedish Brown beans from Greg Reynolds at Riverbend Farm in Delano, MN. Michael Pollan liked it so much he referred to them as the "Magic Beans."

For the Vinaigrette

3 Tablespoons lemon juice
1 Tablespoon Dijon mustard
1 shallot, minced
½ cup extra virgin olive oil

For the Salad

4 cups Swedish Brown Beans, cooked
1 Tablespoon lemon zest
½ cup fresh dill, chopped
Salt and pepper to taste

Serves 4

In a small bowl, mix the vinegar, mustard, and shallot. Slowly drizzle in the olive oil, whisking to emulsify.

In a medium bowl, mix the beans, lemon zest, vinaigrette, and salt and pepper. Allow to marinate 1 hour. Add the dill just before serving.

Chard Salad with Bacon, Beets, and Maple Mustard Vinaigrette

Over the years I've found that the addition of really good bacon is the sure way to get people to eat those often despised veggies like beets, chard, or Brussels sprouts. This salad, with its sweet maple dressing and salty, smoky bacon, has helped many people learn to love beets. When you buy chard and beets, look for a variety of colors. If you buy beets with the tops still attached, wash the leaves and stems and add them to the salad.

To Prep the Chard and Beets

8 small, or 4 large beets, boiled, peeled and cut into 1 inch dice

1 large bunch rainbow chard, well washed, leaves torn and stems chopped

For the Vinaigrette

1 clove garlic, minced

1 Tablespoon Dijon mustard

2 Tablespoons Maple syrup(look for grade B maple syrup in the Co-ops)

2 Tablespoons cider vinegar

¼ cup olive oil

Salt and freshly ground black pepper to taste

6 slices bacon, chopped and cooked until crispy

Serves 6-8

Wash the beets well, and cover in a pan with lightly salted water. Bring to a boil, and simmer until a knife easily pierces through to the middle. This will take anywhere from 20-40 minutes depending on the size of the beets. When the beets are cooked, drain them and cool in ice water. When the beets are cool enough to handle, slip the skins off using a small paring knife. Chop the beets into a 1-inch dice.

To prepare the chard, strip the leaves from the stems and triple wash both, to be sure to get rid of any sand and grit. Dry the chard in a salad spinner, or on paper towels. Tear the leaves as you would tear lettuce for a salad, and chop
. . . continued on page 44

. . . continued from page 43

the stems on the bias to add crunch and color. Mix the greens, stems, and the beets in a large bowl and prepare the vinaigrette.

In a small bowl, mix the garlic, Dijon, maple syrup, vinegar, and olive oil. Season to taste with salt and freshly ground black pepper. Drizzle over the salad and sprinkle with the bacon. Serve immediately.

Caesar Salad

The Campus Club Caesar salads are some of our best selling items in the Servery and the Bar. Serve the salad with grilled chicken breast, flat-iron steak, or salmon that has been seasoned lightly with salt and pepper.

Caesar Dressing (Makes 3 Cups)

1 cup shredded parmesan

1 Tablespoon chopped anchovies

4 cloves garlic

¼ cup Dijon mustard

2 Tablespoons fresh lemon juice

1 ½ teaspoons Worcestershire sauce

½ teaspoon Tabasco sauce

1 ½ cups mayo

1 cup buttermilk

1 ½ teaspoons dried basil leaves

Salt and freshly ground black pepper to taste

For the Salad (Serves 6)

6-4 ounce portions of chicken breast, flat iron steak, or salmon

12 cups chopped romaine

½ medium red onion, thinly sliced

6 hard boiled eggs, sliced

3 cups croutons

½ cup grated parmesan for garnish

Serves 6

In the bowl of a food processor, blend together the parmesan, anchovies, mustard, lemon juice, Worcestershire, and Tabasco. Process until the mixture forms a smooth paste. Put the mixture in a separate bowl, and whisk in the mayo, buttermilk, and basil. Season to taste with salt, and a generous amount of black pepper.

Grill the chicken, steak, or salmon to desired temperature, and allow to rest while you mix the salad.

Toss the lettuce, onion, egg, and croutons in a large bowl with about 1 ½ cups of the Caesar dressing. Top with 4 ounce portions of grilled chicken breast, flat-iron steak, or salmon and garnish with lemon wedges. Sprinkle lightly with parmesan and serve.

Quinoa Tabouli

Tabouli is most commonly made using bulgur wheat, but quinoa, pronounced KEEN-wah, is a good gluten-free substitute. This is a great salad to serve with grilled lamb, steaks, or chicken. Add it to an appetizer platter with feta, olives, and pita for a great first course, or a light dinner.

2 cups quinoa, uncooked

Zest and juice from 2 small lemons

2 teaspoons Tabasco

1 small clove garlic, minced

¼ cup extra virgin olive oil

¼ cup chopped parsley

1 medium tomato, small dice

1 medium cucumber, seeded and small dice

2 scallions, minced

Salt and freshly ground black pepper to taste

Serves 4-6

Bring 4 cups of water and a pinch of salt to a boil in a medium pot. Add the quinoa and boil for 10-12 minutes.

While the quinoa is cooking, mix the lemon zest and juice with the Tabasco, garlic, and olive oil.

Drain the quinoa in a very fine sieve (it will fall through the holes of a coarse sieve!) and add the dressing. Mix thoroughly, and refrigerate until completely cool.

Add the parsley, tomato, cucumber, and scallions. Season to taste with salt and freshly ground black pepper.

Jorge's Steak and Strawberry Salad

This salad is best in late June when Cornercopia sells us their gorgeous strawberries! Try it with the U of M feta. It's amazing!

Serves 6

Dressing

2 large whole strawberries
½ cup plus 3 Tablespoons plain yogurt
¼ teaspoon minced garlic
¼ cup olive oil
¼ cup champagne vinegar
1 Tablespoon Dijon mustard

Using a blender, purée the strawberries, yogurt, garlic, champagne vinegar, and Dijon mustard until smooth. With the motor running, drizzle in the olive oil. Season to taste with salt and pepper.

For the Salad

1 flank steak, approximately 1-1 ½ pounds
1 teaspoon ground cumin
2 cups diced strawberries
½ cup diced tomatoes
½ cup minced red onions
1 cup crumbled U of M feta cheese
2 avocados, diced
1 cup toasted walnuts
8 cups mixed salad greens

Season the steak on both sides with salt, pepper, and cumin. Grill or broil the steak until medium rare. Allow the steak to rest for 15 minutes, and then cut into small cubes. Toss the steak and remaining ingredients in a large bowl. Drizzle with the dressing, and toss lightly. Serve immediately.

Warm Chèvre and Berry Salad

I first ran this salad in the Servery in June of 2010 as a way to feature the amazing greens, strawberries, raspberries, and blackberries grown by Cornercopia. It went over so well that I put it on our bar menu. Scour the local farmer's markets for interesting varieties of greens, and gorgeous fresh berries, or substitute sliced apples and pears in the fall.

For the Dressing
2 Tablespoons champagne vinegar
1 Tablespoon Dijon mustard
1 small clove garlic, minced
5 Tablespoons olive oil
Salt and pepper to taste

For the Salad
4 cups mixed greens (arugula, radiccio, spinach, or fun varieties of lettuce)
2 cups assorted fresh seasonal berries, or other seasonal fruit
½ cup toasted walnuts
4 ounces chèvre (I prefer Donnay chèvre, available at local Co-ops.)
½ cup panko breadcrumbs
2 Tablespoons canola oil

Makes 2 large dinner-size portions

Pour all the ingredients into a small jar, cover, and shake vigorously. Can be stored in the refrigerator for 5 days.

Using your hands, form the chèvre into two medallions, ½ inch thick. Press the panko into the cheese, being sure to coat all sides. Sprinkle each, lightly, with salt and pepper. Assemble the greens on two dinner plates, and arrange the berries and walnuts on top.

In a small non-stick pan, warm the canola oil over medium heat. When the oil is hot, add the chèvre. Brown gently, about 2 minutes on each side, or until golden and crispy. Top each salad with a medallion, and drizzle with vinaigrette. Serve immediately.

Asian Chicken Salad

Serves 4

Marinade
⅓ cup soy sauce
¼ cup sesame oil
1 teaspoon Sriracha
2 cloves garlic, minced
1 Tablespoon honey
1 Tablespoon fresh ginger, minced

4 boneless skinless chicken breasts, each cut lengthwise into 3 long strips

Soak 12 bamboo skewers in warm water for 1 hour. In the bowl of a blender, purée the first six ingredients until smooth. Skewer the chicken onto the skewers, and pour the marinade over the top. Refrigerate for 1 hour.

Vinaigrette
1 Tablespoon honey
3 Tablespoons rice wine vinegar
1 Tablespoon soy sauce
¼ cup sesame oil

Whisk all ingredients together, and set aside.

Peanut Sauce
⅓ cup peanut butter
1 Tablespoon soy sauce
2 Tablespoons rice wine vinegar
1 Tablespoon honey
1 teaspoon Sriracha

Whisk ingredients together and thin with a few drops of water if needed.

. . . continued on page 56

. . . continued from page 55

For the Salad

4 cups cooked rice noodles

½ bunch cilantro, chopped

4 scallions, sliced thin

1 large carrot, grated

1 cucumber, seeded and sliced

2 cups Napa cabbage, thinly sliced

1 Tablespoon each chopped fresh mint and cilantro

¼ cup chopped toasted peanuts

Toss the noodles and veggies with the vinaigrette, and sprinkle with the fresh herbs and chopped peanuts. Grill or broil the skewers until they reach 165 degrees, and then arrange on top of the salad. Brush the skewers with peanut sauce and top with chopped peanuts. Serve the remaining sauce on the side.

Conference Room ABC is a flexible meeting space with panoramic views of the Mississippi River.

Soups

Steak and Potato Soup

This is a great soup to make with leftover steak, pot roast, or any other type of meat you may have on hand.

2 Tablespoons olive oil
1 ½ cups carrots, small dice
1 ½ cups yellow onions, small dice
1 ½ cups celery, small dice
1 quart potatoes, medium dice
½ teaspoon cumin
½ teaspoon cayenne pepper
½ teaspoon minced garlic
6 cups beef stock
1 pound cooked flank steak or other meat, medium dice

Serves 6

Heat the olive oil in a medium pot, over medium high heat. Sauté the carrots, onions, and celery with the cumin, cayenne, and garlic until just softened.

Add the potatoes and stock and boil for 8 minutes or until potatoes are soft. Add the steak and simmer for another 5 minutes.

When the potatoes are cooked through, season to taste with salt and pepper.

Chili

1 Tablespoon olive oil

1 medium onion, medium dice

1 large red pepper, medium dice

1 large green, or poblano pepper, medium dice

4 large cloves garlic, minced

1 pound ground beef, preferably grass fed

1 Tablespoon toasted, freshly ground cumin

1 teaspoon toasted, freshly ground coriander

½ teaspoon cayenne

1 ½ teaspoons hot chili powder

2-24 ounce cans diced tomatoes, with juice (Muir Glen is a good brand.)

1 can tomato paste

1-24 ounce can black beans

1 quart chicken stock

Salt and pepper to taste

Serves 4-6

Put 1 tablespoon olive oil in a large pot and turn heat to medium high. Sauté the onion and spices until fragrant.

Add the beef and brown until cooked through. Add the tomatoes, tomato paste, beans, and enough chicken stock to just cover the ingredients.

Simmer chili for 15 minutes, and add the peppers. Simmer an additional 20 minutes, until the chili is thick. Season to taste with salt and pepper.

Chilled Cucumber Soup

This is the perfect soup to make on those humid 90 degree days in August. No cooking involved!

6 cups buttermilk

2 medium cucumbers, peeled and seeded

½ cup sour cream

2 medium cucumbers, unpeeled, seeded and diced small

1 red pepper, small dice

8 radishes, small dice

1 ½ teaspoons minced garlic

4 scallions, chopped

3 Tablespoons lemon oil, or 2 Tablespoons fresh lemon juice

Salt and white pepper to taste

¼ cup fresh dill, chopped

1 Tablespoon mint, chopped

Serves 4

In a blender, combine the buttermilk and peeled cucumbers. Add the sour cream and purée until smooth.

Pour the mixture into a large bowl and add the diced cucumber, red pepper, radish, and garlic. Stir in the scallions and lemon oil, or juice, salt, and white pepper and refrigerate for 1 hour.

Add the dill and mint just before serving.

The West Wing is the main dining room at the Campus Club.

Entrées

Equadorian Beef Stew

This stew is the creation of our Demi Chef, Johnny Bravo, (yes, that really is his name!) and sells out nearly every time he makes it. It's great in winter as hearty comfort food, but is also wonderful in the summer when local peppers, onions, and cilantro can be found at the farmer's markets.

2 Tablespoons olive oil
1 red onion, julienne
1 yellow onion, julienne
1 green pepper, julienne
1 red pepper, julienne
1 yellow pepper, julienne
1 Tablespoon garlic, minced
1 Tablespoon ground cumin
½ cup red wine
1 pound flat iron or flank steak, cut into 2-inch strips
1 quart of water
¼ cup chopped cilantro
1 cup shredded lettuce
1 large tomato, medium dice
1 avocado, sliced
1 lemon, cut into wedges

Serves 4-6

Heat the oil over medium high heat in a large sauté pan. Add the onions and peppers and sauté until lightly browned.

Add the garlic and cumin, and carefully deglaze the pan with the wine. Add the steak, and stir the meat with the onions and peppers.

Add the water and bring to a boil. Simmer for 10 minutes on medium heat until the water has reduced.

Add the cilantro and season to taste with salt and pepper. Serve over rice (see page 67) with shredded lettuce, sliced avocado, fresh tomato, and a lemon wedge.

Nettie's "Sure to Get Me a Husband" Rice

When I worked at Lucia's restaurant in Minneapolis, my dear friend and mentor, Annette Colon, taught me how to make rice the Puerto Rican way. She guaranteed that if I mastered this recipe, and ever moved to Puerto Rico, I would always be able to get myself a husband!

1 Tablespoon butter or canola oil
2 cups basmati rice
3 cups water
1 teaspoon salt
2 fresh bay leaves

Serves 6

Heat the oil in a medium pot over medium high heat. Add the rice and sauté for several minutes until the rice starts to become golden, and begins to smell like fresh popcorn.

Add the water, salt, and bay leaves. Bring to a boil and cover the pot with foil, and a lid as well. Reduce the heat to low, and simmer the rice for 18 minutes. Fluff the rice with a fork, and serve immediately.

Chicken Curry with Spicy Lentils and Cilantro Chutney

Cilantro Chutney

2 bunches cilantro, washed and stems removed

1 large clove garlic

Zest and juice of 1 lime

¼ cup finely grated, toasted coconut

½ cup canola oil

½ teaspoon Tabasco

Salt and pepper to taste

Spicy Lentils

1 Tablespoon vegetable oil

1 small onion, small dice

2 cloves garlic, minced

1 Tablespoon fresh ginger, minced

1 jalepeño, minced

2 cups lentils, well rinsed

1 bay leaf

5 cups water

¼ teaspoon salt

Serves 4-6

Combine the first four ingredients in the bowl of a food processor. With the motor running, slowly drizzle in the canola oil. Season with Tabasco, and salt and pepper to taste.

Heat the oil in a medium pot, and brown the onion over medium high heat. Add the garlic, ginger, and jalepeño, and sauté for 1 minute. Add the lentils, bay leaf, salt, pepper, and water and bring to a boil.

Cover the pan, and simmer the lentils until soft, about 15-20 minutes. Stir occasionally and add more water if necessary.

. . . continued on page 72

continued from page 71

Chicken Curry

2 Tablespoons sesame oil

4 boneless, skinless chicken breasts, sliced into 1-inch strips

3 Tablespoons good quality curry powder

1 yellow onion, large dice

2 large carrots, peeled, large dice

1 red pepper, large dice

1 small bunch broccoli, cut into florets

2 cloves garlic, minced

2 Tablespoons fresh ginger, minced

1-12 ounce can coconut milk

Zest and juice from two large oranges

Zest and juice from one lime

1 Tablespoon hot pepper sauce

Salt and freshly ground pepper to taste

1 cup plain yogurt

1 cup toasted cashews

Heat the sesame oil in a wok, or large frying pan until just beginning to smoke. Add the chicken and curry powder and stir-fry over high heat for 1 minute. Add the onion, and carrot, and continue to cook for 1 minute. Add the red pepper, broccoli, garlic, and ginger and cook one minute longer. Add the coconut milk, zests, orange and lime juice, and the pepper sauce.

Simmer until the chicken is done, and the vegetables are soft, but not soggy. Season to taste with salt and pepper, and serve over the lentils. Garnish with the cilantro chutney, yogurt, and cashews.

Salmon with Mango Salsa

Try to use Ataulfo mangoes for this recipe. These are the mangoes that are showing up in co-ops and ethnic grocery stores that are yellow, smaller, and generally uglier than the more common green-red mangoes. Don't be afraid! They are much sweeter, and have an almost silky texture. This recipe makes a bit more salsa than you may need for the salmon, so snack on the leftovers with tortilla chips.

Mango Salsa

4 ripe mangos, peeled, small dice
1 small red pepper, small dice
¼ cup minced red onion
¼ cup fresh lime juice
1 Tablespoon lime zest
½ jalepeño, minced
½ cup chopped cilantro
Salt and pepper to taste

Serves 4

Combine all the ingredients in a small bowl and chill for 1 hour before serving.

For the Salmon

1 Tablespoon canola oil
4-6 ounce portions of salmon, preferably wild
Salt and pepper to taste

Season the fish on both sides. Heat the oil in a large non-stick pan over medium high heat. When the oil begins to shimmer, add the fish. Sear for 3 minutes, and turn. Cook the fish for another 2-3 minutes until medium rare. Serve immediately with the mango salsa.

Tostadas

If we go more than two weeks without serving Tostadas in the Servery, I know I will be hearing about it from our regulars! There are a lot of steps and ingredients in this recipe, but it's a great meal to prepare with friends on a Saturday afternoon.

Pico de Gallo

2 large ripe tomatoes, medium dice

2 Tablespoons red onion, minced

½ jalepeño pepper, small dice

¼ cup chopped cilantro

Juice and zest of 1 lime

Salt and pepper to taste

Makes 12 6-inch Tostadas

Make the Pico first so that the flavors can blend while you prepare the other parts of the Tostadas.

Mix the ingredients in a medium bowl, and refrigerate for 1 hour.

For the Beans

1 Tablespoon canola oil

½ medium yellow onion, small dice

2-24 ounce cans black beans, with liquid

2 cloves garlic, minced

1 Tablespoon ground cumin

1 teaspoon ground coriander

1 teaspoon Tabasco

Salt and pepper to taste

Heat the oil in a medium pot over medium high heat. Sauté the onion until browned. Add the beans with the liquid, the garlic, and spices and simmer for 10 minutes. Purée the beans in the bowl of a food processor until smooth. Keep warm, until serving.

. . . continued on page 78

. . . continued from page 77

Beef or Turkey

1 Tablespoon canola oil

½ small onion, small dice

1 pound ground beef or turkey, (We buy Thousand Hills Beef, and Ferndale Market Turkey.)

2 teaspoons ground cumin

1 teaspoon ground coriander

½ teaspoon cayenne pepper

2 cloves garlic, minced

Salt and pepper to taste

For the Tortillas

12, 6-inch flour or corn tortillas (Look for La Perla, a local tortilla company, available at most Twin Cities Co-ops.)

1 quart canola oil

Toppings

Have any of the toppings prepared ahead of time, for serving.

Grated Pepper Jack or Cheddar Cheese

Sour cream

Hot Sauce

Avocado

Shredded Lettuce

Brown the onion in the oil, and add the ground beef, spices, garlic, and salt and pepper. Brown the meat until cooked through, and keep warm until the tostadas are fried and ready to be served.

Tortillas

Pour enough canola oil into a large, deep pot to reach 2 inches up the side. Heat the oil to 325. Add the tortillas to the oil, being careful not to overcrowd them. Fry on each side for 1-2 minutes, or until golden and crisp. Remove the tortillas from the oil and drain on paper towels. Keep the tortillas warm in a low oven, if not using right away.

Serving and Assembly

Serve all the components in separate bowls, so that your guests can assemble their tostadas as they like. Typically, one would start with a tortilla, spread on some beans, top with the meat, the pico, and then other accompaniments you are serving.

Cumin Crusted Pork Tenderloin with Charred Tomatillo Sauce

For the Pork

3 pork tenderloins, cleaned of silverskin

4 Tablespoons toasted cumin seeds, <u>divided</u>

1 ½ teaspoons kosher salt, or coarse sea salt

Freshly ground black pepper

1 Tablespoon canola oil

For the sauce

1 jalepeño

4 poblano chilis, whole

8 tomatillos, husks removed

1 small yellow onion, cut in half

2 cloves garlic

1 Tablespoon sugar

1 bunch cilantro, washed

Salt and freshly ground black pepper to taste

Serves 6-8 people

Using a spice grinder, or mortar and pestle, combine one tablespoon of the cumin seed with the salt. Grind until fine. Rub the tenderloins with canola oil and season with the cumin salt, and pepper. Spread the remaining cumin seeds on a piece of plastic wrap, and roll the tenderloins in the seeds to coat them. Seal the ends of the plastic wrap and allow the tenderloins to marinate in the refrigerator for 2 hours.

The Sauce

On a hot grill, char the jalepeño, poblanos, tomatillos, and onion until evenly blistered on all sides. Remove the tomatillos and peppers from the grill.

Lower the grill temperature, or if using a charcoal grill move the onion to a cooler spot on the grill. Allow the onion to continue cooking until softened 3-5 minutes.

. . . continued on page 80

. . . **continued from page 79**

Place the jalepeño and poblanos in a Ziploc bag and allow them to steam until cooled. This will loosen the skins and make peeling the peppers much easier. Peel the peppers. Place the cooled onion, tomatillos, jalepeño, and poblanos in a blender and puree. Add the garlic, sugar, cilantro, salt, and pepper and purée until smooth.

Taste and adjust the seasoning. If the tomatillos are too sour, add a bit more sugar.

Grill the tenderloins over medium high heat, until they reach an internal temperature of 140 (for medium), about 3-4 minutes on each side.

Reheat the sauce and serve over the tenderloins. Garnish with cilantro sprigs and lime wedges.

Irish Stew with Guinness

We use lamb from Hill and Vale Farm, in Wykoff, MN, which is available at Seward Co-op in Minneapolis.

3 pounds lamb stew meat, (leg or shoulder work best) cut into 1-inch pieces
1 Tablespoon olive oil
1 large onion, large dice
4 carrots, large dice
3 large cloves garlic, minced
1 bottle of Guinness, or other dark beer
1 teaspoon fresh rosemary, minced
2 teaspoons fresh thyme, minced
2 bay leaves
1 quart beef stock
6 medium red potatoes, large dice
½ cup COLD water
½ cup flour

Serves 6-8

Heat the oil in a large soup pot. Add the lamb and sear over medium high heat, until thoroughly browned. Remove the lamb from the pot, and brown the onion, and carrots. Deglaze the pot with the Guinness, scraping up any browned bits. Return the lamb to the pot, and add the garlic, thyme, rosemary, bay leaves, and stock.

Allow the stew to simmer for 40 minutes, or until the lamb is tender. Add the potatoes and simmer for another 10-15 minutes.

In a small bowl, mix ½ cup flour with ½ cup COLD water. Stir the mixture into the stew, and allow to simmer until thickened. Season to taste with salt and freshly ground black pepper.

Beef Bourguignon

This is the recipe my dad has used since I was a kid. I've fooled around using other recipes, but I've found that Dad's is truly the best!

6 strips bacon, chopped

3 pounds beef chuck, cut into 1 ½ inch cubes

2 large carrots, peeled and large dice

1 rib celery, large dice

½ pound frozen pearl onions

2 Tablespoons tomato paste

4 cloves garlic, minced

2 teaspoons fresh thyme, minced

1 sprig rosemary

1 bay leaf

1 quart beef stock

1 pound fresh button mushrooms, halved

1 ½ cups Burgundy

¼ cup flour

2 Tablespoons softened butter

Salt and pepper to taste

1 large bag egg noodles

Serves 6-8

Sauté the bacon in a large Dutch oven until crisp. Remove from the pot, and brown the beef cubes in the bacon fat over medium high heat. Remove the beef and brown the carrots, pearl onions, mushrooms, and celery.

Return the bacon and beef to the pot, and add the tomato paste, garlic, and herbs. Deglaze the pot with the Burgundy, and add the beef stock. Cover the pot and simmer gently for 1 ½ -2 hours, or until the beef is extremely tender.

Just before serving, mix ¼ cup of flour with 2 tablespoons of softened butter. Drop pea sized balls of the mixture into the simmering stew. Bring to a boil, and allow the stew to thicken.

Season to taste with salt and pepper, and serve over egg noodles, or mashed potatoes.

Mustard Panko Chicken with Pesto

We buy chicken from Callister Farm, available on Saturdays at the St. Paul Farmer's Market. The flavor and texture are amazing! You'll never buy grocery store chicken again!

4-4 ounce boneless skinless chicken breasts, pounded to ½ inch thickness
¼ cup grainy mustard
¼ teaspoon salt
¼ teaspoon black pepper
2 cups panko breadcrumbs
¼ cup canola oil
1 lemon, quartered

Pesto
Use whatever greens and herbs are fresh and local for this delicious pesto. Toss it in pasta, use it to garnish steak, and fish, or spread it on a BLT when the tomatoes are ripe!

1 clove garlic
½ cup parmesan cheese
3 cups spinach, basil, parsley, or arugula
¾ cup olive oil
Salt and pepper to taste

Serves 4

Mix the mustard, salt and pepper in a medium bowl. Add the chicken breasts, and using your hands, coat each thoroughly with the mustard. Dip each breast into the panko, and coat well. Heat the oil over medium heat, in a large non-stick skillet. When the oil is hot, add the chicken and brown slowly for about 5 minutes per side, lowering the heat if necessary to avoid burning the panko. Cook the chicken until the internal temperature reaches 165. Allow the chicken to rest for 2 minutes, then top with pesto, and lemon wedges and serve.

Pesto
Pulse the parmesan and garlic in the bowl of a food processor, until finely minced. Add the greens, salt and pepper, and drizzle in the oil, with the motor running. Store the pesto in the refrigerator with a piece of plastic wrap pressed directly onto the surface. Can be stored up to three days.

Walleye with Lemon Caper Tartar Sauce

4-6 ounce Walleye filets
Salt and pepper to taste
3 Tablespoons canola oil

Tartar Sauce
1 cup mayo
2 Tablespoons fresh lemon juice
1 Tablespoon lemon zest
2 Tablespoons capers, drained
2 Tablespoons chopped parsley
1 ½ teaspoons chopped tarragon or dill
¼ teaspoon Tabasco
Salt and pepper to taste

Serves 4

Pat the walleye dry with a paper towel, and season with salt and pepper. In a large non-stick, or cast iron pan, heat the oil over medium high heat. When the oil is hot add the walleye. Resist the urge to turn the fish too soon. Allow the fish to cook about 2 minutes or until a golden crust has formed. Turn the fish gently, and cook for another 2-3 minutes. Serve immediately with tartar sauce and lemon wedges.

Tartar Sauce
Mix all ingredients together in a small bowl and chill 1 hour before serving.

Braised Pork Shanks, Pot Roast. . . Or Whatever Else You Want to Braise

We use this method for many of our recipes. This is how we cook pot roast, short ribs, and pork shoulder. It works best with tougher cuts that have some fat on them, and requires some love and patience. A big part of braising is the stock. Braises always taste better to me when I make the stock myself. If you've got leftover bones, veggie scraps, or herb stems save them in a zipper bag in the freezer until you have enough to fill a pot. Cover the scraps with cold water, add a couple peppercorns and some herbs and let it simmer for 2-3 hours on low. Strain it and use it right away, or freeze it in small batches for a later use.

2 Tablespoons olive or canola oil

4 pork shanks

3 carrots, large dice

3 ribs celery, large dice

1 large onion, large dice

1 long sprig rosemary

3 cloves garlic, whole

1 cup wine (red, white, or whatever is on hand)

1 teaspoon tomato paste

3 bay leaves

3 large sprigs thyme

Approximately 1 gallon stock (beef, or chicken, whatever you've got)

Serves 4-6

Heat the oil in a heavy Dutch oven over medium high heat. Season the meat lightly with salt and pepper, and sear in the oil until all sides are well browned. Make sure not to crowd the meat. Keep an eye on the bottom of the pot, so that it doesn't burn. You want it to be a nice caramel color.

When the meat is seared, remove it from the pot, add a bit more oil if needed, and brown the carrot, celery, onion, and whole garlic cloves over medium high heat. When the veggies are nicely caramelized, add the tomato paste and sauté 1 minute. Add the wine to deglaze

. . . continued on page 92

. . . continued from page 91

the pot, scraping the bottom to release the fond (all the good brown stuff). Arrange the meat and herbs in the pot, and add enough stock to just cover the meat. If your Dutch oven is actually oven-proof, you can cook the meat in the oven at 325 for about 2 hours. Otherwise, you can simmer it on the stovetop on low heat for about the same time. Cooking time can vary dramatically depending on the size of the pieces of meat, but the best way to check for doneness, is to take two forks and pull the meat apart. If it comes apart with no effort, it's ready. If you find yourself tugging at it, even the slightest bit, keep cooking!

When the meat is tender, remove it and the veggies and hold in a covered container to keep hot. Reduce the braising liquid over high heat until it becomes thick enough to coat the back of a tablespoon. Again, the cooking time on this can vary dramatically depending on how much liquid is left to reduce. Once it reaches the consistency you like, add the meat and veggies back in, taste for additional salt and pepper and then serve.

Herb Roasted Chicken or Turkey with Seasonal Fruit Chutney

1 whole chicken, whole turkey, or turkey breast
1 batch of "Use It On Everything," Herb Oil
Salt and pepper to taste
1 batch Seasonal Fruit Chutney

"Use It On Everything," Herb Oil

We make variations of this herb oil to marinate beef, poultry, lamb and fish, on roasted potatoes, sautéed with vegetables, or brushed onto grilled bread. Feel free to use whatever herbs you like-mint, dill, oregano. Play around with flavors, and try it out on all kinds of things.

1 cup canola oil
4 large cloves garlic
1 Tablespoon fresh rosemary
1 Tablespoon fresh thyme
1 Tablespoon fresh parsley
1 Tablespoon fresh tarragon
¼ teaspoon salt
Freshly ground black pepper

Preheat the oven to 350. Rub the chicken or turkey liberally with the herb oil, using enough to coat all sides and under the skin. Season with salt and pepper and roast uncovered until it reaches an internal temperature of 165. Allow to rest 15 minutes before carving, and serve with the chutney.

"Use It On Everything," Herb Oil
Puree all ingredients in a blender until smooth.

. . . continued on page 94

. . . continued from page 93

Seasonal Fruit Chutney

This is a great condiment to offer with the standard Thanksgiving turkey dinner, but is also nice to have around to add to ham, grilled cheese sandwiches, or cheese platters.

2 large cloves garlic, minced

1 1-inch piece fresh ginger, peeled and minced

½ of one jalapeno, seeded and minced

1 pound fruit, large dice (you can use apples, pears, cranberries, rhubarb, or green tomatoes)

¾ cup cider vinegar

¾ cup packed brown sugar

¾ teaspoon salt

1 cinnamon stick

⅛ teaspoon ground allspice

½ cup dried fruit (optional)

Combine all ingredients in a non-reactive pot, and bring to a boil. Lower the heat, and simmer on low for ½ hour, or until the chutney is reduced and thickened. The timing can vary dramatically, depending on how juicy the fruit is. Stir often!

Remove from the heat and add ½ cup raisins or dried cranberries if desired.

Stuffed Crêpes

Makes 12, 8-inch crepes

Crêpe Batter
5 eggs
1 ¼ cups milk
1 ¼ cups water
2 ½ cups flour
3 Tablespoons melted butter
¼ teaspoon salt
1 cup fresh spinach leaves, packed (You could also use arugula, or parsley.)
¼ cup melted butter for cooking the crêpes

Mix the eggs, milk and water in a blender. Add the flour, 3 Tablespoons of butter, and salt and blend until smooth. Add the spinach and blend until the batter turns bright green and you can no longer see bits of the leaves.

Melt one teaspoon of the remaining butter in a non-stick pan over medium high heat. Pour ¼ cup of the crêpe batter into the pan. Swirl the pan to evenly distribute the batter. Cook until little bubbles appear on the surface of the crepe and then begin to pop. Loosen the crêpe with a rubber spatula and flip. Cook for another 30 seconds and remove onto a parchment lined plate. Continue making crêpes until all the batter is used.

Béchamel
5 Tablespoons butter
4 Tablespoons flour
4 cups milk
1 teaspoon salt
Pinch of white pepper

Béchamel
Melt the butter in a medium saucepan over medium heat. Add the flour and stir until smooth to make a roux. Increase the heat to

Filling and Assembly
1 bunch asparagus, blanched
2 cups grated gruyère cheese
2 large red or yellow peppers, julienne and sautéed
2 cups ham, small dice (We use Fischer Farms.)

. . . continued on page 98

. . . continued from page 97

medium and cook for 5 minutes until just golden. Whisk in the milk, adding it slowly, making sure there are no lumps. Bring to a boil, and cook 6 minutes, stirring constantly. Season with salt and white pepper.

Filling and Assembly
Preheat the oven to 350. Lay 3 spears of asparagus on 1 crêpe. Sprinkle with cheese, peppers, and ham. Top with 3 tablespoons of béchamel, and roll the crêpe, tucking in the sides. Repeat with the remaining crêpes. Place the crêpes on a greased baking sheet, top with more cheese, and bake in the oven for 15 minutes. Serve immediately.

The Campus Club offers small meeting rooms for members.

Breakfast

Campus Club Granola

Browse the bulk foods aisle at a neighborhood co-op, or check out the Whole Farm Co-op website before you make this granola. Both carry locally raised oats, flax, sunflower seeds, and maple syrup. When buying maple syrup, look for Grade B. It is less refined and has a deeper maple flavor. Most commercial maple syrup today is actually corn syrup with maple flavoring added. You'll never buy Mrs. Butterworth's again!

2 cups oatmeal
½ cup whole, unblanched almonds
¼ cup sesame seeds
¼ cup whole flax seeds
2 Tablespoons ground flax seed
¼ cup unsalted sunflower seeds
¼ cup canola oil
¼ cup real maple syrup

<u>Campus Club Trail Mix</u>
Make the same granola recipe but add 1 cup chocolate chips, and 1 cup raisins or other dried fruit, after the granola has cooled.

Makes about 4 cups

Preheat the oven to 350, and spray a large cookie sheet with non-stick spray. Mix the dry ingredients in a large bowl. Mix the canola oil and maple syrup in a separate bowl, and then add to the dry ingredients. Toss until thoroughly coated.

Spread the granola evenly on the cookie sheet and bake for 20 minutes. Using a large spatula, toss the granola and return to the oven to bake evenly. Bake an additional 20 minutes, or until the granola is golden brown and evenly toasted. Allow to cool and store at room temperature for up to 3 weeks. Serve over yogurt, or use it in oatmeal cookies.

Amy's Strawberry Bread

This recipe has been in my family since the 1970's, when my mom found it in a local newspaper. My sister, Amy, began baking this bread on a fairly regular basis when she was a little girl, and got so good at it that I always think of it as, "Amy's Strawberry Bread."

½ cup butter
1 cup sugar
½ teaspoon vanilla
2 eggs, separated
2 cups flour
1 teaspoon baking powder
1 teaspoon baking soda
1 teaspoon salt
1 ½ cups frozen strawberries, drained and juice reserved

Makes 1 loaf

Grease one 8 ½ x 4 ½ inch loaf pan, and preheat the oven to 325. In the bowl of a mixer, cream the butter and sugar until light and fluffy, about 3 minutes. Add the vanilla, egg yolks, and one tablespoon of the strawberry juice. Sift the dry ingredients, and add to the butter mixture, mixing just until incorporated. Using a large spatula, fold in the strawberries.

In a separate bowl, beat the egg whites until just stiff. Gently fold the whites into the batter, and pour into the pan. Bake the bread 50-60 minutes, or until a toothpick inserted into the center comes out clean. Cool for 10 minutes and remove from the pan.

Zucchini Bread

During the growing season, Courtney Tchida, of Cornercopia, calls each week with a list of fresh produce. In July of 2009, I began noting the desperation in her voice when she'd read down the list and finally get to zucchini. I'd been using it in everything, and was racking my brain to figure out one more dish I could sneak it into, when she told me that at home she grates it and freezes it in zipper bags for the winter. So over the next two months, my staff began running enormous, 20- inch zucchinis through the food processor and storing it in the walk-in freezer. Gladys Saeteros, who now does much of our baking, began making my mom's zucchini bread recipe to use for breakfast pastry orders. As of July 2010, we had two bags of frozen zucchini left—just in time for the new stuff to come in!

3 eggs
2 cups sugar
1 cup canola oil
2 cups grated raw zucchini
2 teaspoons cinnamon
2 teaspoons vanilla
2 ½ cups flour
½ cup oatmeal
1 teaspoon salt
1 teaspoon baking soda
½ teaspoon baking powder

Makes 2 large loaves

Preheat the oven to 350. Grease and flour 2 9x5 inch loaf pans. In the bowl of a mixer, beat the eggs and sugar until light and fluffy. Add the oil, and zucchini. In a separate bowl, mix the dry ingredients. Add the dry mixture to the wet and mix until just incorporated. Pour the batter evenly into the two pans, and bake for 50 minutes. Cool the bread for 15 minutes and remove from the pans.

Banana Bread

1 stick of unsalted butter
1 cup sugar
2 eggs
1½ cups flour
1 teaspoon baking soda
1 teaspoon salt
1 cup mashed banana
½ cup sour cream
1 teaspoon vanilla

Makes 1 large loaf

Preheat the oven to 350. Grease a 9x5 inch loaf pan. In the bowl of a mixer, cream the butter and sugar until light and fluffy. Add the eggs, one at a time, beating well after each. In a separate bowl, mix the dry ingredients together and combine with the butter mixture until just incorporated. Add the bananas, sour cream, and vanilla. Pour the batter into the pans and bake for one hour. Cool the bread for 15 minutes and remove from the pan.

Scones

Scones are best eaten the day they are baked. If you are prepping them a day or two ahead, wrap the dough in plastic after forming it into a round and refrigerate. Then simply cut and bake the scones the day you need them.

2 cups flour

½ cup sugar, plus 2 tablespoons for sprinkling

1 Tablespoon baking powder

A pinch of salt

1 ⅓ cups cream

¾ cup other (dried fruit, nuts, chocolate chips, or berries)

Shortcakes

Make the same recipe as the scones.

For berry shortcakes add 1 Tablespoon water, and 1 Tablespoon sugar to 2 cups fresh berries.

Makes 6 scones

Preheat the oven to 350. Using your hands, mix the dry ingredients, including the nuts, chocolate or berries, in a large bowl. Add the cream and mix lightly until the dough just holds together. Resist the urge to knead the dough-you'll wind up with tough scones! Gently pat the dough into a 1/2 inch thick round, and cut into 6 triangles. Place the scones on a parchment lined baking sheet and brush with cream. Sprinkle with the remaining sugar, and bake for 7 minutes. Turn the oven down to 300 and bake for 7 minutes more.

For Shortcakes

Cut the rounds into 6-8 triangles. Bake at 350 for 7 minutes, then turn oven down to 300 and bake another 7 minutes. To serve, split the shortcakes in half, horizontally, fill with whipped cream and seasonal fruit.

The Café Bar overlooks the Fountain Terrace behind Coffman with a wonderful vista of the Mississippi River.

Beet the Devil Cake

2 cups puréed beets
4 ounces unsweetened chocolate
1 cup canola oil
3 eggs
1 ¾ cups sugar
1 Tablespoon vanilla
1 ½ cups flour
2 teaspoons baking soda
¼ teaspoon salt

Cocoa Frosting

½ cup plus 2 tablespoons
unsalted butter, room temperature
5 cups powdered sugar
8 Tablespoons milk
1 ¼ teaspoons vanilla extract
¾ cup plus 3 Tablespoons
unsweetened cocoa powder

Beat the butter in the bowl of a mixer until light and fluffy. Add the powdered sugar 1 cup at a time, beating well after each addition. Add the milk, vanilla, and cocoa powder and beat until smooth. Be sure to scrape the bowl so that all the butter is thoroughly incorporated. Spread the frosting between the cake layers and around the outside of the cake.

Serves 12-16

Preheat the oven to 350. Spray 2 8-inch round baking pans with non-stick spray. Line each with a parchment round, spray again and then dust with flour.

Melt the chocolate in a small bowl in the microwave on medium power for 20 seconds. Allow to cool slightly. In the bowl of a mixer, mix the oil, eggs, and sugar on high speed until light and fluffy, about 5 minutes. Add the chocolate and beets. Add the flour, baking soda, and salt and mix until just combined.

Pour the batter in the pans and bake for 30-35 minutes, or until a toothpick inserted into the middle comes out clean. Allow the cakes to cool for 15 minutes in the pan. Turn the layers out, allow to cool completely, and frost with Cocoa Frosting.

Honey Yogurt Panna Cotta

*Panna Cotta is such a pretty, seemingly decadent dessert,
that it's surprising how simple it is to make. In the summer,
top it with fresh local berries, and in the winter simmer dried
fruit with a little wine and sugar for a more seasonal garnish.*

1 cup milk
1 Tablespoon unflavored gelatin
1 ½ cups cream
¼ cup sugar
3 Tablespoons honey
⅛ teaspoon salt
**½ vanilla bean, split and seeds
scraped**
1 ½ cups yogurt

Serves 6

Pour the milk in a medium bowl
and sprinkle the gelatin over the
top. Allow the gelatin to dissolve,
about 10 minutes.

Put the cream, sugar, honey, salt,
and vanilla in a medium saucepan, and warm gently over medium heat, just until the sugar has
dissolved. Do not boil! Remove
from the heat, and stir in the gelatin mixture. Whisk in the yogurt.

Strain the mixture through a fine
mesh sieve to remove any lumps,
and pour into 6 wine glasses or
ramekins. Refrigerate for at least
4 hours, and top with fresh berries
before serving.

Apple Crisp

This recipe can be adapted to use pears, rhubarb, plums or whatever fruit is in season. If using a juicier fruit like rhubarb, or berries, add 2 Tablespoons of flour to the fruit mixture.

10 cups apples, peeled and thinly sliced
1 cup brown sugar
1 teaspoon cinnamon

Topping
1 ¼ cups flour
⅓ cup white sugar
10 Tablespoons cold butter, cut into small pieces
Pinch of salt

Serves 10-12

Preheat the oven to 350. Mix the apples, sugar, and cinnamon and put in a 9x13 inch pan.

Put the dry ingredients in the bowl of a food processor and pulse several times. Add the butter and pulse just until the mixture begins to form small clumps. Spread the topping over the fruit and bake for 40 minutes, or until the apples are bubbling and the crisp is lightly browned.

Mini Cream Puffs

Makes 40

1 cup water
½ cup unsalted butter
¼ teaspoon salt
½ teaspoon sugar
1 cup flour
4 eggs

Glaze
1 egg
1 teaspoon water

Cream
1 cup whipping cream
2 Tablespoons powdered sugar
1 teaspoon vanilla
2 cups assorted berries

Combine the water and butter in a saucepan and bring to a boil. When the butter has melted add the salt and sugar. Using a wooden spoon beat in the flour, stirring to break up any lumps. Continue stirring the dough over medium heat, until a sandy skin begins to appear on the bottom of the pan, about 5 minutes. Move the dough into a medium mixing bowl and stir in the eggs, one at a time, beating well after each egg.

Preheat the oven to 425. Line two baking sheets with parchment paper. Place the dough in a pastry bag fitted with a fluted ½ inch tip, and pipe 1 inch round mounds onto the baking sheets. Brush each with the glaze and bake for 15 minutes, then reduce the heat to 375 and bake another 30 minutes. Cool the puffs before using, or freeze for a future use.

Beat the cream, sugar, and vanilla on high speed until stiff peaks form. Split the puffs horizontally and fill with the cream. Place 2 or 3 berries in each puff, and top with the cap. Dust the cream puffs lightly with powdered sugar.

Meringue Mushrooms

It is best to make these on a dry day-high humidity will kill them! They're great on cookie trays and make a beautiful decoration for a Yule Log.

4 egg whites at room temperature
¼ teaspoon cream of tartar
¾ cup sugar
½ teaspoon almond extract
2 ounces melted chocolate (semi-sweet or bittersweet)
Cocoa powder for dusting

Makes 30

Line two large cookie sheets with parchment paper, and preheat the oven to 200. In a mixing bowl, beat the egg whites and cream of tartar on high until soft peaks form. Sprinkle in the sugar, 2 tablespoons at a time, beating well after each addition until the sugar is dissolved. Beat in the almond extract. The whites should stand in stiff, glossy peaks.

Spoon the meringue into a large zipper bag, or a pastry bag with a medium opening. If using the zipper bag, cut ½ inch off one of the lower corners of the bag. Pipe the meringue onto the cookie sheets into 30 mounds, each about 1 ½ inches in diameter, to resemble mushroom caps. Pipe the remaining meringue upright onto the other cookie sheet into 30 1 ¼ inch lengths to resemble mushroom stems. Bake at 200 for 1 hour and 45 minutes. Turn the

. . . continued on page 124

. . . continued from page 123

oven off and let the meringues stand in the oven 30 minutes longer to dry. Cool completely before decorating.

With the tip of a small knife, cut a small hole into the center of the underside of each mushroom cap. Place a small amount of melted chocolate in the hole and spread the underside of the cap with the chocolate. Attach the stem to the cap by inserting the pointed end of the stem into the hole of the cap. Allow the chocolate to dry, about 1 hour. Just before serving, sprinkle the tops of the mushrooms lightly with cocoa.

Laurie's Never Fail Pie Crust

My mom found this recipe in the newspaper at least 30 years ago, and in my whole professional cooking career, I've never found a better pie crust. It is extremely forgiving, as long as you keep it cold. Don't be afraid to roll it thin. The flakiness and flavor are exceptional! I use it for pies, tarts, quiches, or galettes.

3 cups flour
1 ¼ cup butter
1 egg, well beaten
5 Tablespoons cold water
1 Tablespoon vinegar
1 teaspoon salt

Makes enough for 4-5 galettes or pies.

Mix together the flour and salt. Cut the butter into small pieces and mix into the flour to form a coarse meal.

In a separate bowl, mix together the egg, water, and vinegar. Add to the flour, and mix gently to form the dough. Do not over mix! Form into 4 flat rounds, and chill before rolling.

Apple or Pear Galette

This recipe can be adapted to use pears, rhubarb, plums or whatever fruit is in season. If using a juicier fruit like rhubarb or berries, add 2 additional tablespoons of flour to the fruit mixture.

1 10 inch pie crust, rolled thin (see page 125)

4-5 cups sliced apples or pears

¾ cup brown sugar

1 Tablespoon flour

½ teaspoon cinnamon

2 Tablespoons cream for brushing

1 teaspoon sugar for sprinkling

¼ teaspoon cinnamon for sprinkling

Serves 8-10

Preheat the oven to 425. Lay the pie crust flat on a parchment-lined sheet tray. Mix fruit with the sugar, flour, and cinnamon and place in the middle of the pie crust. Fold the edges up around the fruit.

Brush the galette with cream and mix 1 teaspoon of sugar with ¼ teaspoon of cinnamon. Sprinkle over the galette. Bake the galette for 25-35 minutes or until nicely browned and the fruit has begun to bubble.

Raspberry Sorbet

2 cups water

2 cups sugar

4 ½ cups raspberry purée (strained)

3 Tablespoons lemon juice

Serves 6

Boil the sugar and water for one minute, and cool to room temperature to make a simple syrup. Whisk the simple syrup into the raspberry purée, and add the lemon juice. Freeze in an ice cream maker according to manufacturer's instructions.

Sweet Corn Ice Cream

3 cups cream

1 ½ cups milk

1 vanilla bean, split

6 ears of corn, shucked and corn sliced off the cob and puréed (Reserve the cobs!)

1 cup sugar

Serves 8-10

Heat the cream and milk in a large pot over medium heat. Add the puréed corn kernels, the cobs, and vanilla bean, and simmer gently for 20 minutes. Remove the pot from the heat and allow the mixture to steep for 2 hours. Strain the mixture through a sieve and add the sugar. Cool in the refrigerator for 1 hour. Freeze the mixture in an ice cream maker according to manufacturer's instructions.

Liquid Nitrogen Ice Cream

This is the recipe we used to make ice cream for the Chemistry Department dinners. The liquid nitrogen freezes the mixture instantly and produces the creamiest ice cream ever. Obviously, most people aren't going to have access to liquid nitrogen, but this recipe can be made using a commercial ice cream maker with great results. This is a good base for making other flavors of ice cream. Add nuts, chopped chocolate, or pieces of fresh fruit after churning to make it your own.

Serves 8-10

2 cups of heavy whipping cream
2 cups of skim milk
3/4 cup of sugar
1 tablespoon vanilla extract
2 liters of liquid nitrogen

Mix the cream, milk, sugar, and vanilla in a large bowl. Get a helper to hold the bowl, using oven mitts, while you whisk in the liquid nitrogen. The ice cream will freeze instantly.

If you don't have access to liquid nitrogen, mix the ingredients in a large bowl until the sugar has dissolved. Churn the mixture in an ice cream maker according to the manufacturer's instructions. Add any extra ingredients and put the ice cream in the freezer for another hour until frozen solid.

Note: A common mistake is to churn the ice cream, walk away from the machine, and then let it melt again. If you re-churn the ice cream at this point, you may wind up with butter chunks in the mixture. I often set a timer to remind myself to put the ice cream in the freezer immediately after churning.